Charlie Brown's CYCLOPEDIA

CARS, TRAINS, AND OTHER WHEELS
Rolling Right Along

VOLUME · 5 ·

Based on the Charles M. Schulz Characters
Funk & Wagnalls

Charlie Brown's 'Cyclopedia has been produced by Mega-Books of New York, Inc. in conjunction with the editorial, design, and marketing staff of Field Publications.

STAFF FOR MEGA-BOOKS

Pat Fortunato
Editorial Director

Diana Papasergiou
Production Director

Susan Lurie
Executive Editor

Rosalind Noonan
Senior Editor

Adam Schmetterer
Research Director

Michaelis/Carpelis Design Assoc., Inc.
Art Direction and Design

STAFF FOR FIELD PUBLICATIONS

Cathryn Clark Girard
Assistant Vice President, Juvenile Publishing

Elizabeth Isele
Executive Editor

Kristina Jones
Executive Art Director

Leslie Erskine
Marketing Manager

Elizabeth Zuraw
Senior Editor

Michele Italiano-Perla
Group Art Director

Kathleen Hughes
Senior Art Director

Photograph and Illustration credits:
Courtesy Alfa Romeo, 41; AP/Wide World Photo, 24, 43; Craig Aurness/West Light, 20, 26; The Bettmann Archive, 19; Rich Chenet, 48; Bill Delaney, 26; Steve Dunwell/Image Bank, 56; Cliff Feulner/Image Bank, 30; Courtesy French National Railways, 39; Courtesy General Motors, 49; Rachel Geswaldo, 22; Walter Hodges/West Light, 12, 57; How-Man Wong/West Light, 36; Image Finders, 37; John Kelly/Image Bank, 25; Larry Lee/West Light, 13, 32; Leslie Lovett, 48; Courtesy Peterbuilt, 53; Mary Ellen Senor, 17, 49; Steve Strickland/West Light, 52; Courtesy Suzuki, 45; Courtesy Terex, 54; United States Army, 58; UPI/Bettmann Newsphotos, 43; Anne Van Der Vaeren/Image Bank, 51.

ISBN: 0-8374-0050-3

Part of the material in this volume was previously published in *Charlie Brown's Second Super Book of Questions and Answers*.

Funk & Wagnalls, founded in 1876, is the publisher of *Funk & Wagnalls New Encyclopedia*, one of the most widely owned home and school reference sets, and many other adult and juvenile educational publications.

INTRODUCTION

Welcome to volume 5 of *Charlie Brown's 'Cyclopedia!* Have you ever wondered when the bicycle was invented, or if a car could fly, or which train is the fastest in the world? Charlie Brown and the rest of the *Peanuts* gang are here to help you find the answers to these questions and many more about cars, trains, buses, and trucks. Have fun!

CONTENTS

GOING UP?

CHAPTER 1

Can you imagine a world without wheels? You couldn't take the bus to school. Your roller skates wouldn't roll. There wouldn't be any cars for a ride to the beach or the store. How did people get around before cars were invented?

A WORLD WITHOUT WHEELS

WALKING

How did people travel long ago?

Before people knew of any other way to travel, they walked from place to place. Travel on foot was slow. When people wanted to go long distances, they often had to spend days, weeks, months—even years—getting there.

How were important messages delivered?

People often used special runners to deliver important messages. Once, in ancient Greece, a runner was sent from a city called Marathon all the way to Athens to announce a victory in war. The special 26-mile marathon race that people run today is named after this famous running event from ancient times.

A man recently walked around the entire globe. It took him more than three years to make the trip—including the time he traveled by boat when he came to large bodies of water!

Did rulers and wealthy people in ancient times travel on foot?

Probably not. In ancient Egypt, the Pharaohs (FAIR-oze), or kings, were carried on litters by slaves. The emperors of ancient Rome were also carried this way. A litter was a couch on two poles. Four slaves carried it by balancing the poles on their shoulders. While the slaves walked, the passenger could stretch out on the couch. There were so many litters in Rome, they caused traffic jams!

YOU SHOULD ALL CARRY ME ON A LITTER!

RIDING ON ANIMALS

In Egypt, camels are still used to carry people across the desert.

Why did people first ride on animals' backs?

Large animals such as horses, mules, and camels don't get tired as quickly as people. So when men, women, and children started to ride animals, they were able to travel long distances more quickly than before. They also saved energy by riding instead of walking.

What animals are used to carry people and things?

In the desert lands of Egypt and Syria, people use oxen, donkeys, and camels. Camels are especially good for desert travel because they can live for long periods without water. Reindeer are ideal for the people of icy Lapland, the northern part of Scandinavia. Reindeer move quickly in snow and can carry up to 300 pounds. Eskimos near the North Pole train dogs to pull sleds and carry light loads. In mountain areas, llamas are used because they are good climbers. They carry things for the Indians of Peru in the Andes Mountains.

13

SKIS, SKATES, AND SLEDS

When did people start using skis?

People have used skis for more than 5,000 years. Skiing began as a way of getting around in places where there was a lot of snow. The first skis were probably made from animal bones. Because they are long, flat, and smooth, skis glide easily over snow and ice.

What is cross-country skiing?

When you go cross-country skiing, you don't just go down hills. You may also ski uphill and across flat ground. Cross-country skiers use their leg muscles and swing their arms to push themselves along. They usually ski long distances, often on country trails. Their skis are narrower and lighter than downhill skis. Cross-country skis also have special ridges that grip the snow and help the skier move forward. In places where it snows often, people use cross-country skis to get around.

When did people first ice-skate?

No one knows exactly when people first started ice-skating, but they have been doing it for hundreds of years. Ice-skating was originally a way of traveling. The first ice skates were wooden runners strapped to shoes.

In the Netherlands today, there are many canals that freeze in the winter. People still skate many miles along the canals to get around.

Did people ever use sleds without snow?

Yes, and they still do today. The sled was one of the earliest vehicles. Vehicles are objects that carry people or things from one place to another. The earliest sleds were just flat pieces of wood dragged along the ground. Then people added wooden runners underneath. These were curved like the metal runners on a modern snow sled. Oxen and other large animals pulled the sleds.

Are sleds and sleighs the same?

These words sometimes mean the same thing. They are both vehicles on runners but we often think of a sled as being smaller than a sleigh. People usually use the word *sleigh* to mean a horse-drawn wagon in which people can ride.

What is a toboggan?

A toboggan is a vehicle without runners that glides on snow and ice. A toboggan is made of long strips of wood that curl up at the front. The underside of a toboggan is polished, so it glides easily and moves very fast.

American Indians made the first toboggans to carry things across snow. Today, people use toboggans mostly for an exciting ride down a hillside. There are even special toboggan trails where you can *soar* downhill over hard-packed snow!

15

CHAPTER · 2

It's a perfect circle—
and it's everywhere!
We see wheels under
cars, buses, trucks,
and tractors. Ma-
chines we use every
day need wheels to
work. Clocks, door-
knobs, and egg-
beaters all use wheels!
With the discovery of
wheels, many new
things were in-
vented—especially
vehicles. So let's take
a trip with Charlie
Brown and see how
the wheel gave us ex-
citing ways to get
around.

THE AMAZING WHEEL

WHEELS, WHEELS, WHEELS

Who invented the wheel?

No one knows exactly who invented the wheel or when. We do know, however, that people were using it about 5,000 years ago in the areas now known as Iraq, Syria, and Turkey.

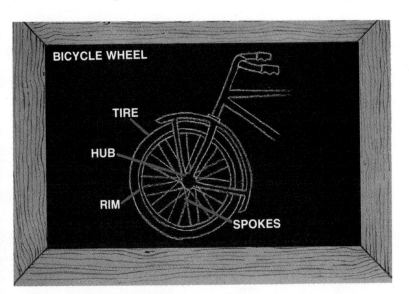

BICYCLE WHEEL

TIRE

HUB

RIM

SPOKES

What are the parts of a wheel called?

Here is a diagram of a wheel. The outer part of the wheel is called the *rim*. At the center of the wheel is the *hub*. The rim is connected to the hub by *spokes*. The spokes are what give a wheel its support.

What was the first wheel like?

The first wheels were probably round slices of a log. The idea for the wheel might have come from log "rollers." People used to place logs under a large object. Then they rolled the object across the logs. There was one problem with this method. As soon as the object passed over a log, the log had to be carried to the front of the object again.

Without the wheel we wouldn't have things such as cars, trains, airplanes, bicycles, watches, clocks, or washing machines!

CHARIOTS, CARRIAGES COACHES, AND WAGONS

What was the first vehicle with wheels?

Probably the chariot. It was a two-wheeled cart, open at the back. At first, chariots were pulled by donkeys. Then people used horses to pull their chariots along. People who rode in chariots did not sit in them—they stood.

Ancient Greeks and Romans used chariots for fighting wars. Sometimes a soldier would stand in the chariot with the horse's reins tied to his waist. Then his hands were free to hold a spear and fight the enemy.

What were other early vehicles with wheels?

Around the same time that the chariot was invented, people started using four-wheeled wagons and two-wheeled carts. These new vehicles were used for carrying heavy loads.

What is a carriage?

A carriage is a vehicle built to carry seated people. Carriages were usually pulled by horses. Ancient Romans used carriages 2,000 years ago, but carriages were most popular in Europe and America in the 1700s and 1800s. During that time, carriages were light, fast, and graceful.

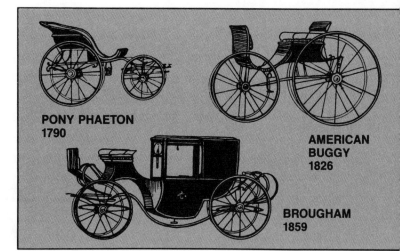

PONY PHAETON
1790

AMERICAN
BUGGY
1826

BROUGHAM
1859

Are there different carriages?

Here are some pictures of a few kinds of carriages. They were all pulled by horses—from one to six, depending on the type of carriage.

How did it feel to ride in a cabriolet?

The cabriolet (cab-ree-uh-LAY) must have given a very gentle, bouncy ride. It was a lightweight carriage, but it had heavy-duty springs under the seat. When a trotting horse pulled the cabriolet over the unpaved roads of the 1800s, the carriage leaped in rhythm.

The French word *cabriolet* means "little leap." It comes from an older French word for baby goat. Riding in a cabriolet probably reminded someone of riding on the back of a playful baby goat.

VICTORIA CARRIAGE

Which carriage did rich people use?

The victoria and the landau were used by rich and royal Europeans. Some wealthy people in America also owned these carriages, which were made of fine woods and metals. From the outside, the landau looked like a jewel box on wheels. Inside, it often had velvet and satin seats and walls trimmed in gold. The landau's roof could be folded back or closed to keep out bad weather.

What was a coach?

Do you remember Cinderella? She rode in a coach when she went to the ball. A coach was a large, four-wheeled carriage that was closed on the sides and on top.

After the 1500s, coaches were used in Europe for public transportation. Rich people owned their own coaches, but their rides were just as bumpy as everyone else's. Early roads were full of holes and bumps, and springs were not put under carriage seats until the late 1700s. Before then, even a king had a very rough ride when he traveled by coach!

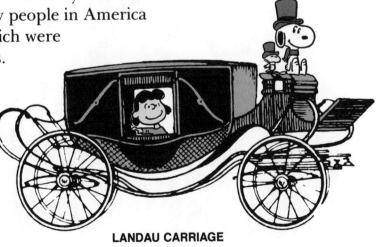

LANDAU CARRIAGE

19

What was a stagecoach?

A stagecoach was a coach that carried passengers. Four to eight people could sit inside the coach. Mail, packages, and luggage were placed on the roof.

Stagecoaches traveled on regular routes between two or more cities. The drivers changed horses at set stops, or "stages," along the routes. That's how stagecoaches got their name. These vehicles became popular in Europe in the late 1600s and in America in the late 1700s. One big problem faced by people who used stagecoaches was the threat of robbers. Poor roads and bad weather also made stagecoach travel uncomfortable and dangerous.

What did American pioneers use to travel west?

American pioneers moved west in covered wagons pulled by teams of horses. True to its name, a covered wagon was a rectangular wooden cart covered by a high canvas top that was stretched over curved wooden ribs. Pioneer families packed their household belongings inside these sturdy wagons. Usually groups of families traveled together. One behind the other, their wagons followed a trail. The long line of wagons was called a wagon train.

Covered wagons traveled in a group called a wagon train.

What is a prairie schooner?

A schooner (SKOO-nur) is a kind of sailing ship, but "prairie schooner" was a nickname for a covered wagon. People called it that because it "sailed" across the prairies or plains just as a schooner sails across the water.

BICYCLES

When were bicycles first invented?

In the late 1400s, the Italian artist and inventor Leonardo da Vinci made the first machine propelled by cranks and pedals, but it didn't look much like the bike you ride today. A French count, Comte Mede de Sivrac (med duh see-VRAHCK), built a wooden model in 1790. It had no pedals and no steering bar. A rider had to move and steer by putting his feet on the ground and pushing. De Sivrac's model was more like a "walking machine" than a bicycle.

In about 1816, a German, Baron Karl von Drais (fon DRICE), built a model with a steering bar. In 1839, foot pedals were finally added by a Scottish blacksmith named Kirkpatrick Macmillan. This bicycle was much more like the ones we see today.

An early bicycle, called a penny-farthing, had a front wheel about nine times larger than the back wheel!

SO, WHO INVENTED BICYCLES, ANYWAY?

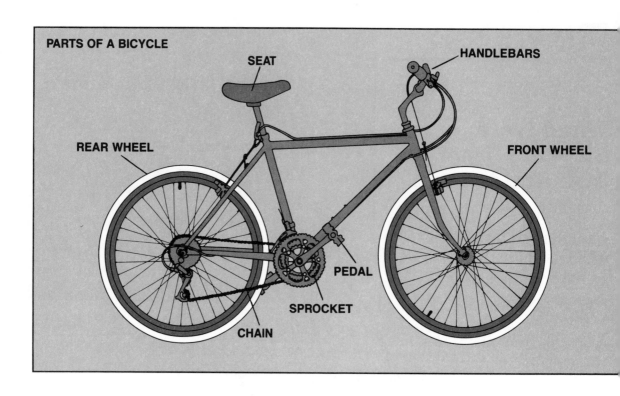

PARTS OF A BICYCLE

SEAT

HANDLEBARS

REAR WHEEL

FRONT WHEEL

PEDAL

SPROCKET

CHAIN

How does a bicycle work?

Between the two large wheels of a bicycle is a much smaller wheel with little teeth on it. This small wheel is called a sprocket. The foot pedals are attached to this sprocket. When a rider pushes the foot pedals, the sprocket turns. One end of a chain is looped around the sprocket. The other end fits around a smaller sprocket in the center of the bicycle's rear wheel. When the large sprocket turns, so does the chain. It turns the small sprocket and the large rear wheel. The bicycle moves forward.

How fast do bicycles go?

The average bike rider can cycle 12 miles an hour. Racers reach 60 miles an hour and more. The fastest bike ride on record was John Howard's 1985 trek across some Utah salt flats. He reached 152 miles an hour!

One man balanced on a bike for 5 hours and 25 minutes —staying absolutely still!

BIKES FOR KIDS

What is a tricycle?

A tricycle is a vehicle with pedals, a steering bar, and three wheels. Most tricycles are low so that young children can climb on easily. Since it has three wheels, a tricycle usually doesn't tip over, so the rider doesn't have to worry about falling. The rider can just climb on, pedal, and have fun!

Training wheels help this rider keep her bike balanced.

Why do people put training wheels on the backs of bikes?

Training wheels keep a bicycle steady and upright. We put them on a bike to help the rider learn how to keep the bike balanced.

A bicycle tips over when it's standing still. It tips over easily when moving slowly, too. It's easier to keep a bike balanced and upright only when it is moving. Training wheels give the bike an extra support on each side. After the rider learns how to balance, the training wheels are taken off.

How do the training wheels work to balance the bicycle?

Try this experiment to see why training wheels work. Stand up straight with your feet close together. Ask someone—someone you trust!—to give you a gentle push sideways. With your feet close together, it's easy to fall over. You probably have to take a step to keep from falling. Now stand with your feet about as far apart as your shoulders. Ask the person to give you another gentle push. This time it is much easier to keep from falling over. With your feet farther apart, you are more stable because you have a wider base. The bicycle is the same. Without training wheels, it tips over easily. But when you attach training wheels to it, you make its base much wider.

Unusual Cycles

What was the longest bicycle ever built?

You've probably heard of a bicycle built for 2. Well, the longest bicycle was built for 35! Made in Belgium, it was taken for a test ride in 1979. The bike weighed more than a ton and was more than 66 feet long. That's longer than ten regular bicycles placed end to end.

This is a bicycle built for 21 people.

What was the smallest bicycle ever built?

The world's smallest ridable bicycle has wheels just over two inches high. Weighing only two pounds, it's so small that it fits in the palm of a man's hand! This tiny bike has wheels made of gold, and diamonds on its pedals. Its owner Charly Charles rides it in Las Vegas, Nevada.

Are there cycles with only one wheel?

Yes, there are. They're called unicycles—meaning that they have one wheel. They're very hard to ride. It takes a lot of practice to learn how to balance on them. You've probably seen circus performers riding unicycles.

What is a mountain bike?

A mountain bike, or all-terrain bike, is a sturdy, heavy bicycle that people started using in the 1980s. The tires of mountain bikes are slightly larger than those on normal bicycles. These bikes are supertough and built to last. Riders take mountain bikes over rough ground and on forest trails where normal bikes might get damaged.

Here's the start of an exciting bicycle motocross!

What is a bicycle motocross?

A bicycle motocross is a type of bike race held outdoors over rugged terrain. The riders use small but tough bicycles to jump over obstacles, climb hills, and weave through moguls (MO-gulls), which are bumps in the ground.

CYCLES WITH ENGINES

What is a motorcycle?

A motorcycle is a two- or three-wheeled vehicle powered by a gasoline engine. Some motorcycles have no engine cover, so the engine is visible between the two wheels.

What is a dirt bike?

A dirt bike is a motorized bike that has a supertough frame and large tires with a wide tread. True to its name, a dirt bike can ride over dirt, mud, and sand. The fenders of a dirt bike are extra high and extra wide. These help protect the driver from the mud and dirt kicked up by the spinning tires. Dirt bike riders need to wear special clothes to protect themselves from injury in a fall, and they must be skilled drivers.

ALL-TERRAIN VEHICLE

What is an ATV?

The letters ATV stand for All-Terrain Vehicle. That means it can ride over rugged land, through the woods, or on a sandy beach. ATVs have four wheels and powerful engines. Since ATVs are very dangerous vehicles, they need expert handling. They should be used only by experienced adults.

26

CHAPTER 3

ALL ABOARD!

Pack your suitcase, buy your ticket, and hop aboard the Snoopy Express. We're off to see old-time trains and modern ones, too. Be sure not even to blink because you might miss the really fast ones. Do you hear the whistle? All aboard!

THE FIRST TRAINS

When did people first start using trains?

The very first trains were used by miners before 1600. These trains had no motors, and they weren't pulled by animals. They were simple wooden tubs that the miners pushed along wooden rails. Later, miners used horses for pulling wagons along the tracks.

Why do trains run on rails?

A vehicle running on rails doesn't hit holes, ruts, mud, or bumps as a car or a wagon on the road does. Pulling a car on rails is easier than pulling a car of the same weight along a road. When a car runs on rails, there is less friction (FRICK-shun), or rubbing, to slow the wheels. So they roll faster and more freely.

YOU HAVE TO PUT THE TRAIN ON THE TRACK IF YOU WANT IT TO RUN.

When was the first railroad built?

The first public railroad was built in England in 1825. It ran along 20 miles of metal tracks. At first the plan was to have horses pull the trains, but the railroad company decided to use steam engines instead. Each steam engine was able to pull a much heavier load than horses would have been able to pull. Because of its powerful engines, the railroad was a great success.

In the United States, the first railroad service began in 1828, using horse-drawn cars. Before too long, however, the American railroad companies switched to steam power.

How fast were the first railroad trains?

In 1830, a British steam locomotive named *Rocket* reached a speed of 29 miles an hour. People thought that the *Rocket* was very fast, and it *was* in those days. Back then the average train moved at a speed of 15 miles an hour.

How did the first trains in America look?

In the 1830s, America's first steam-powered trains were pulled by a car with a steam boiler, a round furnace with a smokestack in the center. Passengers sat in cars shaped like stagecoaches. These coaches were mounted on flat platforms with wheels.

One early train used a sail. The wind moved the train along the rails!

TODAY'S RAILROAD CARS— FROM THE COWCATCHER TO THE CABOOSE

What is a cowcatcher?

A cowcatcher is the iron grill at the front of the first car of a train. The cowcatcher sweeps over the tracks. Its name came from what it was used for—pushing stray cows from the tracks in front of the train.

What is a locomotive?

A locomotive is the railroad car that holds the train's engine. Usually, the locomotive is at the front of a train and pulls it. Sometimes, it is at the back of a train and pushes it instead. People often use the word *locomotive* to mean the engine itself.

The Trans-Siberian Railroad in the Soviet Union is the largest railroad system in the world. Its tracks would stretch from New York to California—and back again!

Why do locomotive engineers use train whistles?

Locomotive engineers use whistles to warn people and animals that a train is coming. They also use train whistles to signal crew members and other railroad workers. "Whistle talk" is a code made up of short and long toots. For example, one short toot means stop. Two long toots means go.

What other safety measures do locomotive engineers depend on to prevent accidents?

Railroads have other safety measures besides train-whistle warnings. One of these is the block signal system. A block is a length of railroad track, usually one or two miles long. To prevent collisions, only one train at a time is allowed in a block. Colored lights signal whether a train may enter a block. Red means stop. Green means go. Yellow means go ahead with caution. Some block signals are hand-operated by railroad people along the line. Other block signals are operated by computers.

Some locomotives have special panels with signals that give the same information as the signal lights on the tracks. If an engineer does not notice a panel signal to stop, the train will stop automatically. Crew members also use two-way radios to speak with faraway stations and train yards. This allows them to warn the train's conductor if there is danger ahead.

What is a Pullman car?

A Pullman car—sometimes called a sleeper car—is a train car with a place for sleeping. The Pullman car was named after George Pullman, one of the first Americans to make train travel more comfortable for passengers. If you had ridden on one of the first Pullman trains, you would have eaten fancy foods beneath the light of crystal chandeliers!

What is a caboose?

The last car of a train is often called the caboose. Long ago it was reserved for the trainmen or owners of cattle. Today the caboose often carries passengers and cargo, just like the other cars of the train.

LET'S GET THIS CABOOSE ROLLING, CONDUCTOR!

FREIGHT TRAINS

What is a freight train?

A freight train doesn't carry passengers. It moves packages, metal, animals, mail, lumber, and other goods from place to place. An average freight train has about 100 cars.

What's the longest freight train on record?

The longest freight train stretched 4 miles. It was made up of 500 coal cars and 6 diesel locomotives—3 at the front and 3 near the middle of the train. Weighing 47,000 tons, this freight train traveled 157 miles on the Norfolk and Western Railway on November 15, 1967.

What types of cars do you find in a freight train?

Freight trains have different kinds of cars to carry different kinds of freight. For example, boxcars carry grain, cans, and packages. Boxcars are enclosed. Flatcars are open platforms used for carrying logs, steel, and machinery. Stockcars carry cattle, pigs, or sheep, so the cars have open slats for the animals to breathe. There are also refrigerator cars for fruits and vegetables, tank cars for oil and milk—and even poultry cars for chickens!

TUNNELS AND UNDERGROUND TRAINS

Why are railroad tunnels built?

Most railroad tunnels are built through hills and mountains. Instead of winding miles and miles of track around a mountain, builders usually cut through the mountain in a straight line. With the help of a tunnel, the train route is shorter— and safer, too!

How is a railroad tunnel built?

It takes a special crew of engineers and experts to build a railroad tunnel. Workers drill holes deep into the side of a hill or a mountain. They pack an explosive such as dynamite into the holes. Huge sections of rock and earth are blasted away in seconds. The workers clear away the loose rock from the explosion, then they drill more holes.

After they have cleared the tunnel all the way through, they line it with concrete. Then they lay down the track. Finally, the railroad tunnel is ready to be used.

© 1986 United Feature Syndicate, Inc.   1-31

SOUNDS LIKE A TRAIN GOING THROUGH A TUNNEL, HUH, MA'AM?

What is a subway?

A subway is a passenger railroad that runs mostly underground. It is powered by electricity. Because it is underground, a subway is perfect for a crowded city. Except for its station entrances, it does not take up any street space. Since subways carry people all around a city, the trains make lots of stops along their routes.

The Tokyo, Japan, subway system hires special workers to squeeze passengers into crowded trains! They wear special uniforms and clean white gloves. Despite their job, the "squeezers" are very polite.

KINDLY, STEP IN, PLEASE.

When was the first city subway opened?

The first subway was opened in London, England, on January 10, 1863. The trains used steam locomotives that burned a type of fuel called coke. The subway smelled so bad, it was nicknamed "the sewer"! The tunnels were so dirty and dark that some passengers carried candles to light their way. But people still used these trains. This first subway carried nearly 10 million passengers in its first year.

How many cities in the world have subways?

There are about 70 subway systems in the world today. Some of the cities with large subway systems are New York, Paris, London, Berlin, Moscow, Hamburg, Tokyo, and Boston. Not all cities call them subways. Some use the name metro, underground, or tube.

The busiest subway system in the world is in Moscow. It may carry 6½ million passengers a day!

35

STREETCARS, CABLE CARS, AND MONORAILS

What is a streetcar?

A streetcar is a vehicle that moves along rails that are set into the surface of the road. Streetcars usually run within city limits.

How were the first streetcars pulled?

In the early years of the twentieth century, streetcars were pulled by horses. The rails made the horses' task easier. At the same time, the passengers got a better ride since the tracks were smoother than the bumpy roads.

How do modern streetcars get their power?

Modern streetcars get their power from electricity. Today there are two kinds of streetcars. One is called a trolley car. Its power comes from an overhead electric line. The other is called a cable car. It is pulled by a heavy steel rope called a cable. The cable moves along a slot under the surface of the street.

How are cable cars used?

Cable cars are used to climb steep hills and mountains. In San Francisco, the hills are so steep that buses and trolleys have trouble climbing them. Cable cars do the job.

What is a monorail?

A monorail is a railroad that has only one rail. This rail may be above or below the monorail cars. Monorails cannot travel as fast as other trains, but they are cheaper, cleaner, and quieter to run.

Canadians use this monorail to get around in Vancouver.

SAN FRANCISCO

TODAY'S SUPER TRAINS

How fast are modern trains?

The average modern train travels at about 65 miles an hour. However, many passenger trains today speed along at 90 miles an hour.

How do modern trains run?

Most modern trains are pulled by locomotives that use diesel-electric engines. A diesel-electric engine is similar to a gasoline engine, but it burns diesel fuel, a kind of oil, instead of gasoline. The diesel turns generators, which supply electrical energy to the electric motors. The motors then turn the locomotive's wheels.

Some locomotives are fully electric. They use no oil. They get electric current from wires hung above the railroad track or from a third rail that runs on the ground inside the track. As with the diesel engine, the electric power turns the train's wheels.

The world's fastest speed for a passenger train was 252 miles an hour, recorded in West Germany in May, 1988!

A MAGLEV DOGHOUSE?

What is the bullet train?

The bullet train is a super-fast electric train in Japan. Called the shinkansen (SHIN-kan-SEN) by the Japanese, it cruises at 130 miles per hour! When two bullet trains pass each other at such a high speed, the air between them is put under great pressure. This causes a loud booming sound. Since the trains have special seals on the doors, passengers don't hear the noise. The bullet train, which carries 100,000 passengers a day, has been running since 1964.

Laid end to end, the world's railroad tracks would stretch 750,000 miles!

What is a TGV?

The TGV is an electrical train in France that's the fastest thing on rails. TGV stands for a French phrase for "very great speed"—and that's what makes this train famous. On a normal day, the TGV zips along at a speed of 170 miles an hour, but it can go as fast as 237 miles an hour!

FRENCH TGV TRAIN

What does *maglev* mean?

Maglev stands for "magnetic levitation." This is a new way to move trains by using electric motors and magnets. The powerful force of the magnets actually lifts the vehicle into the air! Engineers think a maglev train could probably travel as fast as 500 miles an hour.

Maglev trains are not running yet, but scientists in Japan and Germany are working hard on new designs for this speedy train.

CHAPTER 4

Trains made it possible to travel long distances, but they could go only to places where tracks had been built. People were still pulling their carriages and carts with horses, oxen, or donkeys to get to places where trains didn't go. It was pretty hard work—until the automobile came along!

START YOUR ENGINE!

THE FIRST AUTOMOBILES

Who invented the first successful automobile?

EARLY CAR

The first successful automobile was invented in 1770 by a French engineer named Nicolas Joseph Cugnot (KYOU-no). It rode on three wheels and was used to move guns from place to place.

In 1801, Richard Trevithick (trev-EE-thik) built the first automobile to carry passengers.

What kind of engine did the first automobile use?

It used a steam engine. Coal was fired up to boil water and turn it into steam. Inside the engine was a piece of metal called a piston. The steam pushed the piston back and forth. The piston turned a metal rod connected to the car's wheels. When the rod moved, the wheels moved—and so did the car.

Why didn't steam-driven cars last?

NOW I'M REALLY STEAMED!

Most people didn't like steam-driven cars. They filled the air with smoke wherever they went, and hot coals sometimes shot out of the engines! The cars moved slowly—only 10 to 15 miles an hour— but they were so noisy that they frightened both horses and people. In addition, stagecoach and railroad companies did not like the new automobiles. They were afraid that if many people rode in these cars, fewer passengers would ride on their lines. In England, laws limited the use of steam-driven cars. For example, one 1865 law said that a signalman had to walk in front of each car and warn people it was coming!

What does *horsepower* mean?

Horsepower is an old English way of measuring an engine's power to do a certain amount of work in a certain period of time. An engine's horsepower compares it to the number of horses it would take to do the work in the same amount of time.

Who are the "fathers" of the modern automobile?

Gottlieb Daimler and Karl Benz, both German, are considered the fathers of the modern automobile. Working separately, Benz (in 1885) and Daimler (in 1886) developed gasoline engines that worked much like the engines used in cars today. Daimler put his engine into a motorcycle. Benz's engine powered a three-wheeled automobile. The company Karl Benz started is now called Mercedes-Benz.

What was an electric car?

An electric car was an automobile powered by one or more electric motors. The motor got its power from a battery. The battery had to be plugged into a wall socket from time to time to be recharged.

Electric cars were popular in the 1890s and early 1900s. They were clean and quiet and reached speeds up to 20 miles an hour. However, after an electric car had traveled only about 50 miles, the battery died! Because the battery had to be recharged often, people tired of the electric car. Inventors worked to develop a new kind of engine.

In 1896, the automobile was so new and strange, it was shown in Barnum and Bailey's Circus!

HENRY FORD AND THE MODEL T

Who was Henry Ford?

Henry Ford was an American pioneer in the building of cars. In 1913, he introduced the moving automobile assembly line. Each worker on an assembly line did just one small job in putting a car together. The parts were on a moving belt. When a worker finished his or her job, the parts moved along to the next worker.

Before Ford's method, workers spent a lot of time doing complicated jobs, but with the assembly line, factories were able to produce cars more quickly and cheaply than before. Ford sold his cars for less than other carmakers, so more people could afford to own them. Because of Henry Ford, cars became a part of American life.

MODEL T FORD

What was the Model T?

The Model T was Ford's most famous car. The Ford Motor Company built this model between 1908 and 1927. To keep prices down, Ford made only small changes in the Model T each year, and he built the car in only one color—black.

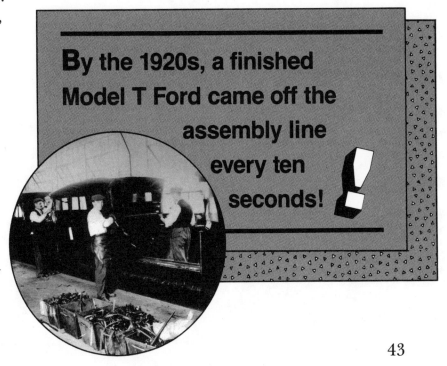

By the 1920s, a finished Model T Ford came off the assembly line every ten seconds!

43

THE GAS ENGINE

How do the engines of our cars work?

When the engine is turned on, gasoline goes to a part of the engine called the carburetor (CAR-buh-ray-tur). There, the gasoline mixes with air. The gas and air mixture moves to the cylinders (SILL-in-durz). These cylinders are hollow spaces inside a solid block of metal.

Inside each cylinder is a piston, a solid piece of metal that moves up and down. The piston moves down to suck in the gasoline and air mixture. Then it moves up again. Just as the piston gets near the top of the cylinder, a spark plug gives off an electric spark. This causes the mixture to explode. Pressure from the explosion pushes the piston down again. This happens in one cylinder after another. These tiny explosions create the energy to move the car.

Can automobile engines run on other fuels?

Yes. Many trucks run on diesel fuel, which is made from petroleum. Engines have to be specially built to burn diesel fuel, and the fuel leaves a dirty residue after it is burned. Another fuel that a car can use is methanol. Methanol is made from grain, and it is used to fuel racing cars. There is also gasohol, a mixture of gasoline and alcohol. Gasohol burns more cleanly than plain gasoline, but it is expensive to produce. Engineers are looking for a cheaper, cleaner fuel for cars of the future.

RULES OF THE ROAD

CAR STEERING WHEEL AND DASHBOARD

How does a driver control a car on the road?

A driver uses the steering wheel to direct the car, and pedals to control the car's speed. One of these pedals, the gas pedal, is connected to the engine. When the driver pushes the gas pedal with his or her foot, the car moves. Pushing the other pedal, the brake pedal, makes the car stop.

The car's lights, heater, windshield wipers, air conditioner, and radio are usually controlled by levers, knobs, or buttons on the dashboard. The dashboard is the long panel inside the car just ahead of the steering wheel. The dashboard also has numbers or dials that light up. They tell a driver how much gas and oil are in the car, and how fast the driver is going.

Why do cars have license plates?

All states require car owners to register their cars. License plates are part of this registration. A license plate can help the police find a stolen car. It can also help identify a car in case of an accident.

States also use car registrations as a way to check the safety of automobiles. Some states require car owners to have their cars checked once or twice a year. Unless the car meets the state's safety standards, the owner cannot renew the car's registration.

Why do you need seat belts and shoulder harnesses in a car?

Seat belts and shoulder harnesses help protect passengers from injury during an accident. They hold a person in place when a car suddenly stops or turns. Seat belts and shoulder harnesses often save lives. Expert drivers use seat belts—and you should always wear yours, too!

What does a speed limit on a road mean?

A speed limit is the fastest safe driving speed on a certain road. On most highways in the United States, the speed limit is 55 miles an hour. This limit is meant to save gasoline as well as lives. When automobiles move at higher speeds, they use more gasoline.

If a car goes over the speed limit, the driver may be stopped by a police officer and given a speeding ticket. The driver then has to pay a fine. If he or she gets too many speeding tickets, the state government will take away his or her driver's license.

Every year more than seven million cars end up in junkyards!

What makes police cars different?

Most cars driven by police officers have sirens and round or bar-shaped lights on the roof. When these are turned on, the noise and flashing lights warn people that the police are near. Other drivers slow down to let the police rush to the emergency.

Most police cars also have two-way radios. When someone needs help, the message comes over the radio to the police officer in the car. Some police cars also have computers. When the officer punches in a license plate number, the computer tells him or her who the car belongs to and if that person has any unpaid tickets. All these facts come from the computer in less than ten seconds!

Super Cars of Today and Tomorrow

What's new in the world of cars?

Since the time of the Model T, car owners have enjoyed automobiles with many new features. We can get air-conditioning, adjustable and heated seats, car phones, and gauges that show the outside temperature and which direction the car is traveling in. Some cars even talk to the driver! They tell the driver when a door is open, or when the car needs gas.

Engineers are working on a car that flashes information—right on the windshield. It can show a map of the car's destination and will even warn a driver if another car is too close!

Why are racing cars built differently?

Racing cars are built for speed and power. Many cars, like those driven in Grand Prix (grahn pree) races, have sleek bodies. They are built narrow and close to the ground. This is so the force of the wind coming at them won't slow them down. Instead, the wind streams over and around the car.

Some racing cars even have "wings" mounted on their backs. These wings, also called airfoils, are not meant to lift the cars off the ground. In fact, they do just the opposite. They push the cars closer to the road, which helps them go faster.

Racing cars also have wide tires, good for going around corners and giving the car stability.

What is stock car racing?

Stock car racing is the most popular motor sport in America. These racing cars look similar to cars driven on the street. Stock car racers start with showroom cars, which they rebuild. On the track, stock cars are awesome, mean-racing machines.

STOCK CAR

What are funny cars?

Funny cars are a type of drag-racing car. A drag race is a short-distance race at super speeds. A funny car's body looks like a regular street car, but it's really only a fiberglass copy. Funny cars have powerful engines built to get to super speeds fast. They race one-on-one, so you won't see more than two cars on the track at any one time.

FUNNY CAR

What are rocket cars?

Rocket cars are the fastest wheels on Earth! They are shaped like a rocket with small wheels underneath and larger wheels behind the rear fin. One of these supercars broke the sound barrier at more than 700 miles an hour! You can tell they are fast by their hot names—*Blue Flame*, *Spirit of America*, *Rocket*, and *Thrust 2*. How do they get their power? From built-in rockets and jets!

Are there cars that run on solar power?

It took powerful brakes and a seven-foot parachute to stop the *Blue Flame* after its 630-mile-an-hour ride! Nine years later, in 1979, the *Rocket* broke the speed of sound at more than 739 miles an hour!

Yes. One is called the Sunraycer and is powered by the heat of the sun! The Sunraycer looks like a blue bubble on four wheels. It's more than 20 feet long and 6 feet wide. Since a solar-powered car runs on sunlight, a rainy day could be a problem for it, but not this one! A battery inside the Sunraycer soaks up the sun's rays so that the car will move even on a cloudy day.

SUNRAYCER

49

CHAPTER 5

BUSES AND BIG RIGS

What would we do without buses to take us to school, through the city—or even across the country? And the millions of trucks on our country's highways move just about anything you can imagine. There's no doubt about it. It takes big wheels to do big jobs!

BUSES

Where does the word *bus* come from?

The word *bus* is short for *omnibus*, which means "for everyone."

What were early buses like?

The first buses were large carriages drawn by horses. One of the earliest buses carried people around Paris as long ago as 1662.

New York City started bus service in 1829 with its "sociable." The sociable was a carriage with enough room to seat ten passengers.

In the same year, the first omnibus rolled down the streets of London. The omnibus was pulled by three horses side by side. This caused terrible traffic jams. The streets weren't wide enough for the omnibus and other traffic, too. Later, these buses were made narrower so they could be pulled by two horses.

DOUBLE-DECKER BUS

Why was the double-decker bus invented?

The London omnibus was very popular. Many people wanted to ride it, but there was not enough room. So some people used to hold on to the roof. Because of this, a long bus seat was added to the roof in 1847. Seats on the open top were half price. Later, a canopy was added to protect passengers from rain and sun. Today double-decker buses run in London, but they have closed tops.

What are the longest buses in the world?

The longest buses in the world are each 76 feet long. That's twice as long as an average bus. These very long buses, used in the Middle East, have room enough to seat 121 people.

TRUCKS!

Why are there many different kinds of trucks?

Different kinds of trucks are needed to do many different kinds of jobs. Refrigerator trucks carry food that spoils if it is not kept cold. Tank trucks carry liquids such as gasoline. Small enclosed trucks called panel trucks carry small packages and mail over short distances. And bottle trucks have special racks for holding cases of bottles.

Here's a big truck on the move.

What is a trailer?

A trailer is a van or wagon that is pulled by another vehicle. It has no engine of its own. Some trailers are boxcars built to carry everything from clothes to furniture. Some trailers are called flatbeds. They are open platforms used to carry heavy machines—or other trucks.

The first postal trucks in the United States were made so that a mule could be hitched to one if the steam engine failed to work!

What is a tractor truck?

A tractor truck, or "rig," is the front part of a big tractor-trailer. It contains the engine and the cab, where the driver sits. The tractor truck can be driven without the trailer, but the trailer can't be driven without the tractor truck because it has no engine of its own. Power for the trailer's brakes and lights comes from the tractor truck.

TRACTOR TRAILER

Are there any other kinds of trailers?

Yes. Some mobile homes are trailers that can be pulled by a car or a truck. Mobile homes are outfitted with beds, seats, and even bathrooms and kitchens. Many people spend their vacations traveling around in trailers. Some people build foundations under their trailers and live in them all the time.

In 1904, there were only 700 trucks being used in the United States. Today, there are more than 12 million trucks on the road in the United States!

CAMP GROUNDS

BULLDOZERS, DUMP TRUCKS, CRANES, AND CEMENT MIXERS

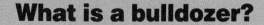

What is a bulldozer?

A bulldozer, or earth mover, is used to clear away trees and spread dirt. This big machine has a giant blade or shovel in front. A bulldozer runs on belts of metal tracks instead of wheels. The tracks spread the weight of the bulldozer over a greater area and keep the machine from sinking into soft ground. Because the tracks are rigid, the bulldozers can ride over rough surfaces easily.

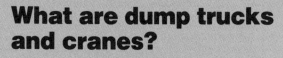

DUMP TRUCK

What are dump trucks and cranes?

Wherever people are building houses or highways, you'll find unusual trucks on the job. Dump trucks have a special open box on the back that tilts so that gravel and dirt can be poured out of it. Cranes also are used at most building sites. A crane has a long arm able to lift heavy objects. Cranes run on long, flat belts, called tracks, rather than on tires. That way they don't get stuck in mud or gravel.

What are cement mixers?

Cement mixers are trucks that carry a giant barrel filled with cement. This barrel rotates on the back of the truck. The cement is poured through a narrow chute.

54

FIRE ENGINES AND AMBULANCES

What were the first fire trucks like?

The first fire trucks were just water pumps on wheels. These pumps were pulled to fires by horses or men. In the early 1800s, American fire companies used steam engines pulled by men or horses. Fire companies tried to outdo one another by hiring artists to paint beautiful scenes on the sides of their engines. They gave the engines fancy names such as *Live Oak* and *Ocean Wave*.

Fire horses of the early 1900s were well trained. As soon as the fire alarm rang, the horses trotted out from their stalls by themselves and stood ready in front of the fire trucks!

What is an engine truck?

When the fire alarm sounds today, fire trucks rush to the scene. One type of fire truck, the engine truck, arrives with its own booster tank of water. This water will be used if the fire fighters can't hook up their hoses to a hydrant (HIGH-drant), a water pipe on the sidewalk, or to a stand-pipe, a large faucet on the outside of some buildings.

What is a superpumper?

A superpumper is a mighty rig with the power to shoot water as far as 1,000 feet away. It can even reach fires in skyscrapers! With a superpumper's help, fire fighters don't have to get close to a fire to put it out.

Which fire truck carries the ladders?

A ladder truck, or aerial (AIR-ee-al) truck, carries ladders that work electrically. This special equipment helps fire fighters reach rooftops and upper stories of buildings to put out fires and rescue people. The ladders are 100 feet long and can reach up to the tenth story of a building. Many lives have been saved with the aerial ladder and with the cherry picker.

What is a cherry picker?

A cherry picker is a traveling crane. It has an arm about 75 feet long, with a big metal bucket on the end of the arm. The cherry picker's bucket carries fire fighters up to rooftops or high windows. Sometimes people trapped in burning buildings climb out of windows and into the big bucket. The crane then lowers them to the ground, where they can climb out to safety.

Fire fighters also use the cherry picker to put out fires in very old buildings. If there is a chance the old building will fall down, the fire fighters spray the fire from the bucket of the cherry picker. This way, if the building collapses, the fire fighters will be safe in the cherry picker.

What were the first ambulances like?

The first ambulances were probably horse-drawn carts. The Spanish army used them as long ago as 1487 to carry its wounded off the battlefield. Before that, armies probably used litters and stretchers to carry wounded soldiers.

What are modern ambulances like?

Most modern ambulances are about the size of vans or small trucks. Inside, they are like traveling hospitals. Ambulances carry medical equipment to treat people who are sick or have had an accident. Specially trained people ride in ambulances to care for the patients during the trip to the hospital.

AMBULANCE

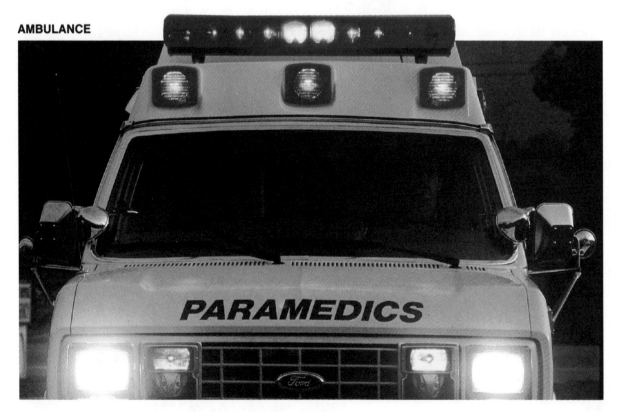

DID YOU KNOW...?

ARMY PORTABLE BRIDGE

● When an army needs to get across a river quickly, there's only one way to go—on a portable bridge! Although this vehicle looks like a tank when it's traveling, it's really an instant bridge. Its platform can unfold to span a 60-foot river. After the soldiers and equipment have gone over it, the instant bridge folds up and moves on again—until the next river!

● What's that in the sky? Not a bird—but an amazing flying car! For years inventors dreamed of a vehicle that would grip the road, then take to the air over traffic jams. Some of these flying cars were actually made and some really worked—but not very well. That's because planes need to be lightweight to work well, and cars need to be heavy to do their job on the road.

● Escalators are moving stairways. The first escalator was introduced in Paris in 1900. Today, the longest escalator, in Leningrad, the Soviet Union, has 729 steps!

I SEE YOU RAN INTO ANOTHER FLYING CAR...

- Some sidewalks move. They are really belts of rubber that carry people along flat surfaces or up slight slopes. These sidewalks help the flow of crowds through long airport or museum corridors, and they sure beat walking!

- Imagine a dump truck that can carry a load weighing as much as 88 cars—or 2,000 people! One monster-sized dump truck can do just that!

And what does this mountain-mover look like? It's as tall as a medium tree and as wide as three Cadillacs—and it's thirsty. It takes 500 gallons of gas to fill up its huge tank!

- Big 18-wheeled tractor-trailers usually zoom along superhighways, but the trailers can also ride "piggyback" aboard railroad flatcars. Traveling this way, the trailers can go long distances without tying up the highways or using gasoline!

- Early elevators were powered by steam engines or pressure from water or oil. Today most elevators are run by electricity—and they can give you a pretty fast lift! The elevators in Tokyo's Sunshine 60 building travel upward at more than 20 miles an hour!

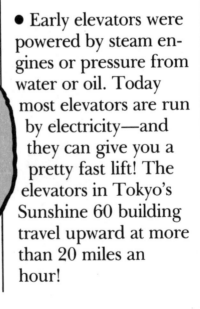

GOING UP?

59

◆ IN THE ◆
NEXT VOLUME

Have you ever wondered how a toaster knows when to pop up, or where escalator steps go after they disappear, or who invented the zipper? You can find the answers to these questions and lots more in volume 6, *How Machines Work— Gears, Gizmos, and Gadgets.*